ETIQUETTE FOR MEN

ETIQUETTE FOR MEN

A BOOK OF MODERN MANNERS AND CUSTOMS

BY

G. R. M. DEVEREUX

CHANCELLOR PRESS

First published in 1929 by C. Arthur Pearson, Ltd

Reprinted 1937

This 2002 edition published by Chancellor Press,
an imprint of Bounty Books, a division of
Octopus Publishing Group,
2—4 Heron Quays, London E14 4JP

Reprinted in 2002, 2003

ISBN 0 7537 0413 7

Printed in Finland by WS Bookwell

* Please note this is a facsimile edition therefore titles mentioned on the back
of this book may no longer be in print.

CONTENTS

FOREWORD

IN these days social affairs are conducted in a rather less formal and conventional manner than was the case even a few years ago. Yet there is still a very definite code of conduct laid down— a code which must be observed to the full by any man who wishes to appear, and to feel, at home in all social circumstances.

In order that the young man of to-day may have an opportunity to know the latest rulings on all matters of etiquette, this book—for many years a standard work of its kind—has been thoroughly revised. The manners and customs which are accepted in all circles as being entirely correct and up-to-date are duly set out in this new edition.

Etiquette is designed simply to assist in the smooth-running of our everyday affairs, friendships, and social functions. For this reason a good knowledge of its rules materially assists any man who desires social happiness and success.

CHAPTER I

EVERYDAY ETIQUETTE

When Travelling—Raising your Hat—Meeting a Lady—
In the Street—Your Umbrella

CONSIDERATION for others at all times is the keynote
of etiquette. It is therefore during our ordinary,
everyday affairs in particular that we show whether
or not we possess the spirit of true courtesy.

The man who appreciates the spirit as well as
the letter of etiquette does not reserve his best
manners for special occasions, or for particular
individuals.

You may know that you are doing the right
thing at all times when offering little courtesies to
others, especially to ladies, whether you know them
or not. You should be ready to vacate your seat
in a crowded vehicle, not only for a lady, but also
for an elderly man.

When travelling with a lady, you should allow
her to precede you on to the vehicle. You should
leave the vehicle first, however, so that you may
assist her to alight. Should your companion be

given a seat by another man, be ready to offer a word of thanks.

Do not seat yourself in a vehicle so that you occupy more than the allotted space, refrain from staring at the passengers seated opposite, and do not read another man's paper.

Raising your Hat

It is not necessary for you to raise your hat if you see a lady of your acquaintance in a public vehicle in which you are also a passenger. A little smile or nod is sufficient.

Otherwise, you should always raise your hat when meeting a lady whom you know. If the lady is a close friend, raise your hat immediately she gets near; but if you do not know her very well, you should wait until she acknowledges your presence before raising your hat.

You should also raise your hat when meeting a male friend accompanied by a lady, whether you know the lady or not; when walking with a lady who meets someone she knows, and when walking with a man who has occasion to raise his hat.

To raise one's hat, however, does not constitute an introduction. If, for example, when walking with a friend you meet an acquaintance of his and raise your hat, you should make no sign if you meet the lady again when alone—unless she should happen to smile or bow.

A final word about hat-raising: While there is no need for a sweeping movement like that of the cavalier of other days, do not go to the other extreme and simply touch the brim with your forefinger, as many men have a habit of doing in these days. Raise the hat just clear of the head for a moment; that is the correct procedure.

Meeting a Lady

You should try to avoid offering a lady your gloved hand. When therefore you see a lady approaching with whom you will wish to shake hands, remove your right-hand glove in readiness. But if you have no time to remove the glove, do not keep the lady waiting while you do so. Shake hands immediately, offering a word of apology for your glove.

When you meet a lady whom you know, and you wish to speak to her, do not keep her standing still. You should walk with her in the direction in which she is going.

You should not offer a lady your arm when walking with her, unless you are escorting her across a busy street.

You should always take the outside of the pavement when walking with a lady. You should also take the outside when walking with two ladies—you should not walk between them.

A smoker should always remove his pipe or cigarette when speaking to a lady, and if walking with a lady he should not smoke without first asking her permission.

When walking with three or more friends, do not walk abreast if by so doing you force other people to walk in the gutter. Walking-sticks and umbrellas should always be carried in such a way as not to inconvenience other pedestrians.

On a wet day you may offer to share your umbrella with a lady who is without one. Some ladies are averse from accepting this courtesy from a man whom they do not know, however; so you should not feel unduly rebuffed if the offer is refused.

If information is requested by a stranger—regarding, for example, the whereabouts of a certain road—show a readiness and real desire to be of assistance. And do not be sparing with a word of apology if you inadvertently cause discomfort to other persons by jostling them or touching them with anything you may be carrying.

CHAPTER II

INTRODUCTIONS

How Introductions are Made—What to Say—Shaking
Hands—At a Party—Letters of Introduction

MANY men are a little shy of making introductions.
They believe there is a great deal of formality about
the matter, and they can never be sure they are
acting in the correct manner.

Actually, to make an introduction is extremely
simple. All you have to remember is that

A gentleman is presented to a lady,

A single girl to a married woman,

A young to an older man.

The phrase used when making the introduction
should be brief. "Miss Brown, may I introduce
Mr Smith?" does very well.

When introducing two of your personal friends,
of your own sex, the phrase may be still less formal.
"Jack, this is my friend, Tom Smith—Jack Brown."

Where the people are of the same sex, and much
of an age and social standing, it is immaterial which
name is mentioned first.

17   2

Always mention the names clearly when making an introduction. Your friends will feel awkward if they are uncertain how to address each other.

If you wish to introduce a newcomer into a circle of friends—at a party, for example—mention the name only. Do not keep saying: " May I introduce——"

If the newcomer is a lady, do not take her round the room to be introduced individually. Two or three of the men nearest should be introduced, other introductions being made as opportunity offers.

Never interrupt a conversation to introduce a newcomer.

When you are walking with a friend, of either sex, and meet someone to whom you wish to speak, you please yourself whether you make an introduction or not. If you do not wish to make the introduction, you should ask your friend to excuse you for a moment before leaving his or her side. Your friend should then walk on slowly. Your stop should be as brief as possible.

Shaking Hands

When you are introduced to a lady, it depends upon her whether you shake hands. The handshake is not general when the introduction is made in the street, though it is usual, except on very formal occasions, when made in the house.

In all circumstances, however, the matter rests with the lady, and you should make no movement to shake hands before the lady offers hers. Men usually shake hands at all times.

You should raise your hat when introduced to a lady out of doors, and your right-hand glove should be removed, in case the hand is offered. Indoors, you should never remain seated when a lady is introduced, though you need not stand to be introduced to another man, unless he be an elderly man, or a man of high position.

When introduced, your first remark should embody the name of the person to whom you have been introduced: "How do you do, Mrs Brown?" The remark, "I am pleased to meet you," is not now used.

When introduced to a lady at a dance, party, or other function, you must remember, if you see her again, that recognition must come from her. You should not raise your hat, or make any sign, until she either nods or smiles at you.

At a party, you need not wait for an introduction before speaking to any other men present, but you should not enter into general conversation with any of the ladies until an introduction has been given.

Some people are a little nervous when first introduced. If you are introduced to anyone who suffers in this way, try to start the conversation going without any awkward pauses. A few simple remarks will usually put the other at ease.

A final word. You should never make an introduction unless you believe that the people concerned will be mutually glad to know each other. If you have the slightest doubt on this point, you should make tactful inquiries beforehand.

Letters of Introduction

Occasionally, introductions are made by means of letter. You might wish to introduce a friend travelling to a distant town to another friend of yours who lives there. Or you might wish to introduce one friend to another in this way over a business matter.

The introductory letter should be handed to the bearer unsealed, so that if he wishes he may read it. The bearer should seal the letter before delivering it, however.

Where the letter serves as an introduction for social purposes you should state that the bearer is a friend of yours and that you will appreciate any kindness shown to him while he is, say, visiting the recipient's town.

If the introduction is for business purposes, you should simply write:—

"To introduce my friend, Mr Brown, who wishes to see you on a matter of business."

The bearer of a social introductory letter should leave it at the house of the person to whom it is addressed, together with his card or a covering note bearing his address. He should not try to deliver it personally to the addressee, but should await the coming of a letter asking him to call.

Where the introduction is for business purposes, the letter may be delivered direct, so that an interview may take place immediately, or a convenient time arranged between the persons concerned.

CHAPTER III

VISITING

THERE are certain points of etiquette to be regarded, even in the least ceremonious circles, when visiting friends. It is bad form, for example, to call uninvited at a meal time. In a small household it may not be convenient to provide for a guest at a moment's notice, and you will place your friends in an awkward position if you call at such a time.

Also, you should avoid calling on friends without invitation if you have any reason to believe that other guests may be present. If you should make a chance call and find there are other visitors, your stay should be very brief.

Usually, you will be invited to leave your hat in the hall; otherwise you will keep it in your hand— you will never, of course, keep it on your head while in the house.

At no time when visiting should you sit down

until you are asked to do so, nor should you smoke without a definite invitation to do so if you wish.

Do not study the contents of the room, or comment on anything it may contain, unless your opinion is invited.

Should lady guests arrive during your visit, rise from your seat when they enter the room, and remain standing until introduced. If the ladies leave before you, you should stand while they are making their departure.

The Tea-table

The etiquette of the dining-table is dealt with at length in a later chapter, but a few words may be said here of the etiquette of the tea-table.

When other visitors are present, whether tea is served at the table or with the visitors seated round the room, it is your duty to offer to assist the hostess by attending to the wants of the ladies present.

The pouring out of the tea is the signal for the meal to begin, and you should then pass the bread and butter, or whatever the fare may be, to all the ladies near you. Afterwards you help yourself. If tea is not being taken at the table, you must find a convenient spot in which to place your cup and saucer when attending to the requirements of the ladies.

If you are the only visitor, you should not help yourself to anything without the invitation of the hostess. As you are the only visitor she can give you undivided attention, and it is for her, therefore, to attend to all your wants.

Parties

When invited to a friend's house for any little function, be sure to arrive punctually. If you are late you may cause a meal to be kept waiting. On the other hand, do not be unduly early; your host and hostess may not be ready for you.

When invited to a wedding, birthday party, or other event to celebrate which you would like to give a present, arrange for the present to be delivered at the house beforehand. It is not strictly correct to take the present with you.

Be ready to take part in entertaining the guests, if you have ability in that direction, without undue pressing. And give courteous attention to the efforts of others.

When leaving a friend's house, do not keep anyone chatting on the doorstep.

Should your wife have visitors, it is your duty to see to the comfort of the male guests while your wife looks after the ladies. You should see to the disposal of coats and hats. If the guest will be staying the night, you should accompany him to his bedroom, to see that he has everything necessary for his use and comfort.

Country-house Visits

If you are invited to stay with friends for a week-end or longer period, to a country house or town residence, be sure to take with you everything you will need during the stay. Do not take unnecessary luggage, but do not be without anything so that you are forced to borrow from your host.

If invited for any particular kind of sport, take the necessary gear with you—racquet, golf clubs, or whatever may be necessary.

If a time for arrival was not suggested in the invitation, notify your friends what time they may expect you, so that they will be in readiness. During your stay adapt yourself readily to the programme of the household, and do your share to see that everything goes smoothly.

Keep to the exact time arranged for your departure. It is the worst of bad form to hint that you would like to prolong your stay. Even if urged to stay longer, do not accept if you know that by so doing you will upset any arrangements previously made by your host and hostess.

Within two or three days after returning home, you should write to express thanks for the hospitality extended to you. The letter should be quite brief—a few simple words of thanks being much better than a lengthy epistle. Something along the following lines serves excellently:—

" DEAR——,

" You will be glad to know that I had a comfortable journey up to town after leaving you on Monday last.

" May I take this opportunity to thank you very, very sincerely for the warm welcome you gave me to your house and for the thoroughly enjoyable time I had during my stay with you. I enjoyed every minute of it.

" Again thanking you,

"Yours sincerely,

" JOHN SMITH."

Visiting Cards

Visiting cards are not used very largely now for social purposes among men. Most men like to have cards, however, and they are convenient for acquainting anyone who may wish to know it with your address.

A man's visiting card must be of the standard size and style. It should measure three inches by one and a half inches, and should be a plain card, without gilt edges.

Either an initial or the full Christian name should be used, but it must be preceded by "Mr."

Mr J. Smith

or

Mr John Smith

is the correct form—not "*J. Smith,*" or "*John Smith.*"

If you have two Christian names, it is usual for one only to appear in full:

Mr John C. Smith,

or

Mr J. Charles Smith.

Although not incorrect to use the right-hand lower corner for the address, the left-hand corner is preferable.

The name should be in "copper-plate," which resembles handwriting, but the address may appear in any kind of ordinary small type.

Joint cards are not now used for a husband and wife; each should have his or her own.

CHAPTER IV

ATTENDING A DANCE

Public Dances—Your Partner—Semi-Private Dances—
Programmes—Private Dances—General Hints

DANCES may be divided into three main classes: Public dances, which you attend, simply by buying a ticket, without perhaps knowing another person there; semi-private dances, such as those held by a club or business house; and private dances, attended only by invitation.

The same general rules of etiquette apply in all cases, but there are one or two special rules applicable to each class of dance.

Public Dances

Probably you will take your own partner to a public dance, and there is no reason why you should not dance with her exclusively if it is your mutual wish.

You should not dance with another lady unless your companion has a partner; you must not leave her to be a "wallflower" while you are dancing.

It is not usual for the M.C. or stewards to make introductions at a public dance, and therefore you are at liberty to approach any lady present to ask for a dance. If she has a male companion, you should speak to him first with a remark such as, "Do you mind if I ask your friend to dance with me?"

You should invite the lady with whom you have the interval dance to take refreshments with you. If you have a companion you should be sure to save the interval dance for her. If alone, you should not ask this dance of any lady accompanied by a male friend. It is his prerogative.

Semi-Private Dances

At a dance of this kind, where probably most of those present know each other, it is very bad form to dance only with one partner.

If you take a companion, you should give her a fair share of attention. You should have with her the first, interval, and last dance. The remaining dances should be divided between your companion and the other ladies present.

If programmes are provided, immediately on arrival note the dances you are having together. Your companion will then be able to fill in the vacant dances as requests for a dance are made to her.

A husband usually has the first dance with his wife. Beyond that, there are no particular dances they need have together, the idea being that each shall be ready to dance with those who otherwise would be without partners. The husband should not book the interval dance, however, until his wife is sure of a partner for that dance.

Private Dances

An invitation to a private dance should be accepted or refused immediately, in order to assist the hostess in her arrangements.

Your first duty, after depositing your coat and hat, is to greet your hostess. Early in the proceedings you should ask your hostess for the pleasure of a dance with her, although her duties may prevent her from accepting. The invitation to dance should also be extended to daughters of the hostess.

Introductions are necessary at a private dance before you may ask any lady you do not know to dance with you. Such introductions are usually made by the host, hostess, a member of their family, or, if there be one, by the M.C.

At the conclusion of the dance you should take leave of your hostess, and express a word of thanks.

General Hints

The following rules apply to dances of any kind:—

Do not offer your arm to a lady when entering the dance-room or when crossing the floor between dances. You may offer your arm when escorting a lady to her seat at the end of a dance number, but this custom is on the decline.

You must not leave your partner to go alone to her seat; you should remain with her until her next partner appears, or at least until the time comes when you must seek your partner for the next dance.

If a lady whom you ask to dance is engaged, or for any other reason refuses, do not ask any other lady seated nearby. She may feel that she is being asked only as a stopgap.

You owe it to your partner at least to appear to enjoy the dance. And don't, unless specially invited to do so, act as instructor.

You should escort back to the hall any lady with whom you take refreshments. You need not remain with her, however, nor need you ask for the next dance.

If you have to leave before the dance comes to an end, first seek out any partners with whom you have engagements, and offer a word of apology and explanation.

Do not keep a partner waiting until after the

music has started.   You should join her before the band strikes up.

Be ready to apologise if you collide with other dancers, and also be ready to accept with good grace the apologies of anyone who happens to collide with you.

Accommodate your style of dancing to that of your partner. If she knows only simple steps, do not try to make her do any elaborate movements.

Don't take up the centre of the floor, don't dance in such a way as to inconvenience other dancers, and don't try to do the latest variation of the waltz or other dance where most people prefer the simple, old-fashioned style.

Suggestions as to the most suitable style of dress for dances of various kinds will be found in a subsequent chapter.

CHAPTER V

AT THE THEATRE

Booked Seats—Your Coat and Hat—Conversation—
Between the Acts—Refreshments—End of the Play

WHEN taking a lady to the theatre you should, if possible, book seats. To stand in a queue until the doors open, and then to sit in the theatre for some time before the performance starts, is tiring, and consequently detracts from your companion's full enjoyment of the play.

If you have booked seats, however, do not arrive at the theatre after the curtain has gone up. To do so means that you are almost certain to inconvenience and annoy those occupying seats in the same row. Try to arrive fully five minutes before the curtain is due to rise. You then have time to settle comfortably in your seats, and dispose of any coats and wraps you may have with you, before the lights are lowered.

Should your companion wish to leave her wraps in the cloakroom, await her return in the nearby lobby. If you wish also to dispose of your coat and hat, do this in the meantime, but do so without delay in order that the lady may not be kept waiting your return.

If you are taking your coat and hat with you into the auditorium, remove your hat at the entrance. It is better to remove your top-coat before going to your seat. At all events, do not wait until the curtain is just going up, and then cause discomfort to those in adjoining seats by struggling out of your coat.

Whether an attendant is showing you to your seats or not, you should precede the lady. Having reached the correct row, you should stand aside for your companion to go to her seat first. Obtain a programme before taking your seat, if possible. This will do away with the necessity for the programme-seller to reach your seat afterwards. It is usual for the man to provide a box of chocolates for his companion on such occasions.

It is, of course, permissible to carry on a conversation until the overture, but it is extremely discourteous to those seated near to talk when the orchestra is playing, or during the progress of the performance. If you happen to have seen the play before, do not spoil the enjoyment of others by unfolding the plot.

Do not hold up the action of the play by excessive applause. It is disconcerting to the actors to have to remain quiet because members of the audience here and there are still applauding.   It is also wrong to endeavour to insist on an encore in a musical play, unless it is quite evident by their applause that the majority of those present wish it.

Between the Acts

It is very discourteous to leave your companion alone during the intervals between the acts while you visit the refreshment room.

If you are alone or with other men it does not matter so much, perhaps; but when you are with a lady you should not readily leave her to her own company.

At most theatres lemonade and similar light refreshments are brought round during the intervals, and you should ask your companion whether you may obtain refreshment for her.

In the case of a matinee, tea will probably be available.   It is usually as well to order this when taking your seat; the attendant will then have it ready for you at the right moment, thus avoiding delay.

At the end of the play assist your companion into her wraps, or wait for her while she visits the cloak-room.   If you have a car waiting, or are engaging a taxi, allow the lady to wait in the vestibule until the car reaches the door.

In most theatres ordinary morning dress may
be worn whatever seats you are occupying. In
important London theatres, however, evening dress
is more usual if you are occupying a seat in a box
or in one of the front rows of the stalls.

CHAPTER VI

PUBLIC DINNERS

Dress—Finding your Seat—Toasts and Speeches—When
to Smoke—Private Dinners—When to Arrive—After
the Dinner

MANY business houses, sports clubs, and societies of
various kinds hold an occasional dinner. Usually
such a dinner is attended, not by invitation, but
by the purchase of a ticket. The procedure, however, is similar to that of a private function except
that there will be a chairman instead of a host.

At the moment, dinners at which men only will
be present are in mind. Except for really big
functions, ordinary clothes are usual, and the
phrase "morning dress" will generally appear on
the ticket.

In any case of doubt, get into touch with the or-
ganiser, as you will feel conspicuous if you appear
in the wrong clothing.

On arrival, go straight to the cloakroom and
deposit your coat and hat. Guests usually assemble
in an ante-room adjoining the room in which the

dinner will be served. Here you may talk with any other guests, whether you know them or not.

Occasionally a chart will be found in the ante-room, showing the position of each guest's seat. If this be so, find where you are placed.

The chairman will lead the way into the dining-room at the correct time.   If you know the position of your seat, go straight to it.   Where there is no chart, your position may be shown by a ticket on the table, and you should walk quietly round until you find your seat.   Where seating is not arranged in any way, you may sit where you wish, except in the seats adjacent to the chairman's seat, which are usually reserved for his friends or guests of honour.

If invited to take a seat near the chairman, accept the honour immediately with a word of thanks.

When you have reached your seat, remain stand-ing by the chair until the chairman is seated.

You may talk to the guests on either side with-out introduction.   Keep silent, however, when the chairman is saying grace.

Unroll your table-napkin and lay it across your knees; do not tuck it in your waistcoat. You are then ready for the first course. Hints on how to deal with the various courses appears in the next chapter.

If wine is included in the price of the ticket, the waiter will serve you in due course. Otherwise the wine steward will attend to your wants, and you will settle your liabilities with him. Another guest may ask you to share a bottle, in which case you must be ready to share the cost, unless he stipulates otherwise.

When toasts and speeches are a feature of the function give courteous attention to the speakers. It is extremely bad form to continue a conversation, even in an undertone.

Smoking is not permitted until the King's health has been drunk. Following the drinking of this toast the chairman will usually announce: "Gentlemen, you may smoke."

Private Dinners

An invitation to a private dinner should be accepted or refused immediately. After an acceptance has been sent, the engagement should never be broken except through entirely unavoidable circumstances such as an illness or a bereavement. The hostess will have gone to great pains to "balance" her guests, and the absence of one may seriously inconvenience her.

You should arrive about ten minutes before the appointed time, the idea being that all the guests shall be assembled a few minutes before dinner, which should be served at the time mentioned on the invitation.

The host and hostess will make any introductions necessary, at the same time letting you know which lady will be your dinner partner.

The host will lead the way to the dining-room with the lady whose rank, social importance, or age entitles her to this preference, the hostess coming last with the most important male guest.

Ladies at once take their seats, but the men remain standing until the hostess has taken her seat.

You will seat yourself to the left of your partner, and, although you may converse with anyone near, your partner should receive your chief attention.

If there are menu cards, be ready to state your preference. Start on each course immediately it is served; it is not now the custom to wait until everyone is served before commencing.

It is only on very formal occasions now that the ladies retire from the dining-room at the end of the meal, leaving the men to smoke and talk together. Usually they remain to smoke a cigarette themselves, after which a general move is made to the drawing-room.

Before leaving, a word of thanks should be expressed to the hostess for the hospitality enjoyed.

CHAPTER VII

ETIQUETTE OF THE TABLE

The Cutlery and Silver—The Glasses—Through
the Courses—The Dessert—Finger-bowls

THOSE who are accustomed to a simple style of
living may be a little uncertain how to proceed
when attending a public or other formal dinner for
the first time. The amount of cutlery and silver,
and the number of glasses, set for each guest seems
almost bewildering.

Actually you can settle down to enjoy the meal
without the least concern. You will find the
apparently formidable business of dining to be quite
simple.

With regard to the silver and cutlery, remember
that the various knives, forks, and spoons are laid
in the order in which they will be required, beginning
with those on the outside.

Should the dinner start with *hors d'œuvres*, the
necessary knife and fork will be handed to you with
the plate. If soup comes first the spoon for this
will be laid first on the right-hand side.

Next, to your right and left you will find the knife and fork, usually of silver, for the fish course, and then a fork or knife and fork for the entrée. Following will be the large knife and fork for the meat, poultry, or game course, a spoon and fork for the sweet, and finally a knife for the cheese. Sometimes a knife and fork are laid for the dessert, though more often these will be given to you with the dessert plate.

The glasses for your use will be found to your right hand. The smaller wine-glass is for sherry, usually taken with the fish. Then there will be a small tumbler or a wide-bowled, stemmed glass, in which you will take Burgundy, hock, or claret. The slender-stemmed glass with a wide, shallow bowl is for champagne, taken after the entrée. There will also be a wine-glass for port, and a tumbler if whisky is being served.

You need not trouble about the glasses, however. The wine is invariably served by a waiter, and he will pour it into the correct glass.

There is no reason why you should take wine, if you do not wish to do so. Ask the waiter for mineral or plain water, according to your preference.

Now let us go through the courses.

Hors d'œuvres

These consist usually of such items as sardines, olives, anchovies, and perhaps oysters. You may be served by the waiter or parlour-maid, though more likely you will help yourself from the dishes on the table, taking a small portion from each dish according to your taste.

Whenever possible, *hors d'œuvres* should be eaten with the fork only. This rule, to use only the fork, without knife or spoon, should be observed throughout the courses.

Oysters are eaten whole, the complete oyster being lifted to the mouth with the fork. The shell should not be raised from the plate, but should be kept steady with the left hand.

Soup

Soup should be taken from the side of the spoon, and drawn into the mouth without noise. If you wish to tilt the soup plate, tilt it slightly away from you. But it is better not to raise the plate at all.

Bread should not be broken into the soup. It should be broken with the left hand as required, and eaten between mouthfuls of the soup. If tiny squares of toast, or *croûtons*, are served, these should be dropped gently into the plate.

Fish Course

If the fish course consists of whitebait, the tiny fishes should be eaten whole. There is no need to try to remove the heads and tails.

Usually fish is served filleted, but, when a portion is served with the bone, do not fillet it yourself before starting to eat. Remove each portion from the bone as you are ready to eat it.

Should a bone reach the mouth, remove it from the lips with the aid of the fork.

Entrees

These generally consist of patties, cutlets, sweetbreads, or perhaps curry. Again only the fork should be used whenever possible, as in the case of patties. Curry should preferably be eaten with the fork only. A spoon may be used if really necessary, but not a knife.

Poultry

When you have been supplied with poultry—or meat or game—do not start until you have been served with vegetables or salad. If poultry or game is served with bone, cut each portion from the bone as you are ready to eat it; do not cut away all the meat beforehand. Bones should not be removed to another plate. A slice of meat should not be trimmed beforehand. If there is any part you do not wish to eat, cut it away as you come to it.

When salad is served on a separate plate, it should be eaten from the second plate, not removed to the meat plate. If asparagus is served with the meat, it is now correct to eat it with the aid of the knife and fork. It need not be lifted with the fingers, as was formerly the case.

Sweets

Use the fork only, if possible, though a sweet such as fruit salad, custard, and similar dishes demands the use of a spoon as well. You should not use the spoon alone.

When stone fruit is served, the stones should be removed on the plate. If a stone should be placed in the mouth, however, remove it with the aid of the spoon.

Sometimes a savoury will be served in place of cheese after the sweet, or in place of the sweet itself. These savouries may be morsels of fish, game, or white meat, or perhaps a preparation made from cheese.

If cheese is served it should be cut with the knife and lifted to the mouth on a piece of bread or biscuit—not with the knife.

Dessert

Pears and apples are held on the dessert fork and neatly peeled with the dessert knife. The fruit should then be cut into quarters, and into smaller portions, and eaten with the aid of the fork. Pineapple is eaten with the dessert knife and fork, while melon is eaten in the same way, or with a fork and spoon.

Peaches, large plums, and the like are skinned first with the knife, being held on the fork during the process. The fruit is then halved, the stone removed on the plate, and the fruit eaten with a fork.

Grapes are placed in the mouth singly, or, rather, squeezed into the mouth, the skin being kept in the fingers. Many people remove the seeds with the fingers, but strictly the fork should be used.

Bananas are simply peeled with the knife and fork, cut into sections, and eaten with the fork.

Oranges are very difficult to manipulate. The skin has to be scored in quarters with the knife, the fruit being held in the hand. The skin should then be drawn downwards with the knife. The pips should be removed from the fruit while it is on the plate. However careful you may be, there is danger that someone will receive a little of the juice, and really the fruit is best avoided at a public dinner.

Finger Bowls

These will probably be handed round with the dessert plates. If this happens, the bowl should be left where placed until the fruit has been eaten. Then the fingers should be dipped lightly in the bowl, one hand at a time, and dried with a touch of the table-napkin.

When you have finished, bunch up the napkin lightly, and place it on the table. Do not fold it.

All the dishes will be offered over your left shoulder. When the servant is at your right shoulder, therefore, you will know that he is serving your neighbour.

Do not be nervous. The odds are that you will get through the dinner without making the slightest slip. If you do make some slight error, however, it will be unnoticed unless your lack of self-possession calls attention to it.

CHAPTER VIII

SPORTS AND GAMES

" Unwritten Laws "—Winning and Losing—Umpires and Referees—" Mixed " Games—Indoor Games—Playing for Stakes—Whist Drives

THE golden rule in sport of any kind is always to "play the game." If you remember this, you will have no difficulty in obeying the many little "unwritten laws" of sport as readily as the established rules of the game.

One of these "unwritten laws" is to win or lose with the same good grace. If you win, do not comment upon your opponent's futile efforts, or call attention to your superior play. If you lose, refrain from belittling your opponent's victories by saying that you are off form, or that your luck is out.

If at any time you happen to be losing, lose well: do not play wildly in order to end the game quickly. Anyone who does this shows not only a lack of control, but also great discourtesy to the opponent.

Always play up well to a partner or the other members of a team, and do not become irritable or sulky if a mistake is made. Be ready, also, to applaud good play on the part of an opponent.

Umpires and Referees

Another important rule is to obey without question the decision of an umpire or referee, whether you agree with that decision or not—and not only to obey the decision with good grace, but to uphold it.

Quite likely the decision is correct. At all events, the umpire is there to regulate the game, and you only obstruct its progress if you also wish to give decisions.

You should obey the umpire's ruling even if the decision has been given in your favour, in your opinion in error. In tennis, for example, it is wrong to drive a ball into the net because you feel that an undeserved point has been given to you. To do so is a direct insult to the umpire, and also to your opponent, who will not appreciate being presented with a point in this manner.

When playing in "mixed games" with ladies, such as tennis or hockey, play in your usual manner. Do not play a "soft" game; the average girl resents the implied suggestion that she is necessarily an inferior player and must therefore be favoured.

Refrain from giving advice on the game unless you are asked to do so, and—in tennis for example—do not try to play your partner's game as well as your own unless your assistance is specially invited by a weak player.

Indoor Games

The unwritten laws mentioned above in connection with outdoor games apply equally to indoor games such as cards, billiards, and so on. And in all cases the rules governing the particular game being played must be adhered to strictly.

A question which occasionally arises in connection with indoor games is that of playing for stakes. If you are in a friend's house, remember that the decision rests largely with your host. If it is your mutual wish to place a small stake on the game, well and good. If, however, your host is not in favour you should not press him in any way. Nor is it correct to press any others who may be present to play for stakes if they have no ready wish to do so.

It must also be remembered that any losses

resulting from the game should be settled immediately play ends.

Public Whist Drives

So far as the play of the cards is concerned the ordinary rules of whist, of course, hold good. Mention may be made of one or two points in connection with these drives, however, for the benefit of those who are not quite familiar with the way in which they are conducted.

First, introductions are not necessary at a public drive, and you are quite at liberty to speak to anyone playing at the same table.

Notices are invariably displayed, either on the walls of the hall or on the tables themselves, as to the method by which players move from table to table at the conclusion of each hand. Sometimes the winning couple move, sometimes the losing couple—the gentleman going to one table, the lady to another. As the method varies, you should acquaint yourself with the procedure of the particular drive before starting to play.

Do not try to rush the game, but on the other hand try not to allow it to drag or the whole progress of the drive may be held up.

Do not talk while the hand is being played, and do not comment on anyone's play to another person.

It is courteous to ask a lady partner in the hand played immediately before the interval if you may obtain refreshments for her, although if she is with friends she will probably wish to take refreshments with them.

CHAPTER IX

MOTORING MANNERS

Courtesies of the Road—Hand Signals—When you have
Passengers—Riding with a Friend—Motor Coaches

IT may be taken for granted that practically every
motorist and motor cyclist is familiar with the laws
and regulations governing the use of the road.
These laws and regulations are set out very clearly
in the various motoring journals and handbooks,
and especially in the booklet which is handed to
every motorist with his licence.

The average motorist, therefore, will be aware
of the discourtesy to other road users—apart from
the danger—in such actions as cutting in, over-
taking at corners or bends, in leaving his car where
it inconveniences other traffic. He will also be
aware that it is a dangerous error to overtake on
the wrong side, or to pull up suddenly without
warning in front of another vehicle. If necessity
arises for a sudden stop, an endeavour should
always be made to warn those approaching from
behind.

Our concern here, however, is more with the simple courtesies of the road—with the little unwritten laws which some motorists are apt to overlook through thoughtlessness or indifference.

A common instance of this thoughtlessness is the possession of an unnecessarily loud horn or siren, and its use in such a way as to scare other road users and pedestrians. Further, many motorists will sound their horn continuously when they wish a vehicle in front to make way for them, without troubling to consider whether the driver in front *can* give way to them.

It is also thoughtless to sound the horn outside a hospital unless it is really necessary to do so. A driver should slow down so that, in the ordinary way, he has no need to give warnings.

The thoughtful motorist will not speed along near the kerb on a wet day, and thus bespatter passing pedestrians with mud. Nor on a fine day will he drive along a country road so speedily as to cover the pedestrians in a cloud of dust.

A motorist should always be careful to give the recognised hand signals when necessary to indicate his intentions. It is not correct to give these signals indiscriminately—if you are signalling you should endeavour first to make certain that other road users are in a position to act in a manner you desire. You should not take it for granted, and work on the belief that other traffic must look after itself.

Be ready to acknowledge signals given by others. If, for example, a warning signal is given from behind you, be ready to indicate in the accepted manner if the vehicle can safely overtake you.

You should keep as much as possible to the side of the road. Now and again one meets a motorist who will keep in the centre, regardless of the more speedy cars behind whose drivers wish to overtake. When passing to the side of the road, however, be careful not to "crowd" cyclists or others into the gutter.

Do not try to force your way through a group of people waiting to board a tram or other vehicle, and be sure to slow down when passing restive horses or other animals. When descending a hill be ready to give way to vehicles coming up.

The foregoing are merely a few of the little courtesies a motorist should bear in mind. There are many others, but once a motorist gets into the way of considering the safety and convenience of other road users, he will do all he can to help "the good fellowship of the road" instinctively.

A final word. Be ready to help any other motorist who is in difficulties, even if it does mean a little inconvenience or delay.   And be sure to respect the rights of others in the garage and when parking.

Passengers

Unless the design of the car is such that you must take your seat first, you should first see to the comfort of anyone riding with you.   Similarly, when possible, you should get out first in order to help your passengers to alight.

If it can be avoided, do not put a lady or an elderly man in the dickey seat.

If you have a nervous passenger, drive slowly and with extra care.   Actually it may be as equally safe to drive fast as to drive slowly, but the nervous passenger does not realise this.

When taking friends for a long drive, remember to pull up occasionally so that they may obtain any refreshment they desire.

Those who do not own cars should be careful not to presume on the good nature of a friend who does own one.

When riding with a friend, do not try to help him to drive—by drawing attention to traffic ahead, for instance, or people crossing the road in front. The odds are that he saw what was occurring ahead long before you did, and your remarks, however helpful you may intend them to be, only serve to distract his attention and to irritate him by reflecting on his driving skill.

Motor Coaches

The etiquette of motor-coach travelling is much like that of train travelling. There is no need to enter into conversation with other passengers seated near. If, however, another passenger shows desire for conversation, he should not be rebuffed. If you happen to be travelling alone, and desire to talk to anyone near, a remark about the weather or a comment regarding the trip you are taking will at once show whether a readiness for conversation is evident.

The above remarks apply to any ordinary short trip of perhaps a few hours. Motor-coach tours, during which the passengers are together for a whole day or perhaps for several days, are a feature of present-day life. When entering the coach for such a tour it is courteous to pass the time of day with your fellow travellers. If you are spending the night at an hotel, you can please yourself, according to circumstances, to what extent you mix with the other passengers; but you should not deliberately remain aloof in any way.

If during a motor-coach trip you pull up for refreshments, you should ask any unaccompanied lady seated near if you may obtain anything for her, but you should allow her to pay for her refreshments without demur.

Do not be unduly noisy in the coach, and do not call out or comment on anyone you may pass. Above all else, refrain from throwing anything over the side of the vehicle.

CHAPTER X

JOINING A CLUB

Method of Joining—Study the Rules—On the
Committee—Visiting a Club

EACH club—social, political, or sporting—has its
own little customs. There are a number of general
rules, however, that are observed in practically
every club, and if you intend or wish to become
a member of any club you should bear these in
mind.

Usually the procedure to join a club is not by
direct application for membership, but by introduction. It will be necessary for a friend who is
already a member to propose you, and, in many
cases, for another member to "second" your proposed admission. You will be notified in due course
by the secretary whether you have been accepted
by the committee. If accepted, you should remit
the necessary subscription and entrance fee before
making use of the club premises.

'It is generally advisable to visit a club on one
or two occasions as the guest of a member before

joining, in order that you may be certain you will feel "at home" there if admitted to membership.

In certain cases a period of "probation" is the custom before a man is admitted to full membership.

Upon becoming a member you should make it your business to familiarise yourself immediately with the rules of the club. Your behaviour during the first month or two of your membership will have a considerable bearing upon your "standing" and popularity in the club afterwards.

It is invariably an understood thing that members are on speaking terms without the formality of an introduction. You should not be unduly shy at conversing with other men. On the other hand, do not thrust yourself forward. It is much better to drift into the easy friendship that characterises the relationship between the members of most clubs.

You should not take advantage of your membership to ask business or similar favours of other members; nor should you endeavour to persuade members to use their influence in any outside matter on your behalf. In many cases a man's club is his refuge from business and other concerns, and you will be breaking at least an unwritten law if you try to intrude business affairs.

You will be expected to pay your subscription

promptly as it becomes due, and you should settle any dining-room, card-room, or other debts immediately they are incurred.

It is the duty of every member to preserve the property of a club, such as furniture, fittings, books, and so on. And above all a member should always so conduct himself as to maintain the dignity and good name of the club.

The Committee

If at a later date you are invited to join the committee of your club, be sure before accepting that you are in a position to fulfil all the calls upon your time which the honour imposes.

At committee meetings help to maintain the discussions on a courteous and business-like footing. The ordinary rules of debate come into operation, and however strongly you feel on the matter you should never display undue feeling. All remarks must be addressed to the chairman of the meeting. You must not break in while another member is speaking, and if you find yourself out-voted on any matter, you must accept the decision of the majority with good grace. Refrain from criticism of the ideas or actions of other committee men outside the precincts of the committee room.

The interest of the club must always be put before any personal considerations.

Visiting

If you are not a member but are invited to visit a club as a guest, remember that your host will be held responsible for your conduct.

Upon arriving—if you are meeting at the club—you should ask for your friend at the door, or at the office inside, or ring the visitor's bell, according to the custom of the club. You should not go in to look for your friend.

As a rule it is not customary for a visitor to address members without an introduction, though you may converse freely if a member addresses you. Your host will make any introductions he may consider necessary, and you should not press for an introduction to any particular member.

You must not attempt to pay for any refreshments or meals: that is entirely your host's concern.

CHAPTER XI

THE ART OF CONVERSATION

Need for Tact—Habits to Avoid—Personal Affairs—General
Hints—Self-consciousness—Subjects for Conversation

IT is during conversation that the opportunity for
the exercise of real courtesy most often arises.

We know that a man is judged to a certain extent
by his appearance. But the judgment that is
passed on his style of conversation is much more
final. For this reason a man is well advised to pay
attention to all the little laws that come into
operation when he is conversing with others.

If we bear in mind that conversation is the art
of exchanging ideas we shall escape many of the
worst pitfalls. There is no exchange of ideas if
one man monopolises the conversation, or if he will
discuss only those subjects that interest him alone.

Tact is essential. The man who always "speaks
as he feels" may be very candid and straightfor-
ward, but it is not long before he says something
which hurts the feelings of those with whom he is
speaking.

Out of consideration for other people's feelings it is advisable to avoid certain subjects, such as religion and, generally, politics. A frank discussion on either of these subjects can be full of interest, but very often such a discussion develops into a heated argument which may end in loss of good feeling.

A man is entitled to uphold his views. But he should endeavour to do so without losing his good humour. Where this is not possible, controversial subjects are better left alone.

Habits to Avoid

One habit that must be avoided is that of breaking in when someone else is speaking. However clever or amusing may be the remark you wish to make, you must keep it until the other person has finished.

Another habit to be avoided is that of suggesting words for another to use and of finishing sentences for those who are slow of expression.

It is very bad form to correct anyone's grammar or pronunciation. It should never be done, even indirectly, by the use of the same word or phrase spoken in the correct manner.

To speak about yourself to any extent, or to discuss your personal affairs in general conversation, are two other things that must be avoided. Nor is it good form to discuss the personal affairs of anyone else.

Finally, it is inadvisable to discuss mutual friends with anyone. Even if your remarks were kindly, they may go back to the person concerned in a distorted manner, and so cause ill-feeling. Apart from that, another person's affairs are purely their concern, and not a fit subject for conversation.

Conversation should not take place while an entertainment of any kind is proceeding, and in no circumstances should you break in on other people when they are conversing on what may be a private matter. Wait until there is a pause in the conversation before you join them.

Speech in General

With regard to speech in general, always use simple language. Flowery expressions, catch-phrases, and foreign words should be avoided.

Conversation may be lively, but it should never be noisy. It is not good form to talk in loud tones, though on the other hand it is equally bad to mumble your words or to speak in such quiet tones that your listeners have to strain their ears, or keep asking you what you said.

When talking with others, don't be self-conscious or shy. If you concentrate on what you are saying, you will soon forget about yourself and

5

the shyness will vanish. Similarly, a habit of hesitating, or of groping for the right word, is another form of nervousness that will soon go if you fix your mind on what you want to say.

It is never difficult to find subjects for conversation if you take a normal interest in current events. Do not devote yourself to the study of one subject, with the idea that you will always be able to fall back on that when conversation languishes. It is a short-cut to the reputation of being a bore.

At all times be ready to do your share of listening as well as talking.

The correct way in which to address people of rank or title appears in a later chapter.

CHAPTER XII

LETTER-WRITING

The Stationery—Care with Dates—Forms of Address—
Closing Phrases — Third-person Communications —
Letters of Condolence—Congratulations

WE cannot always spare the time necessary to write long and interesting letters. We must not overlook the fact, however, that to send a hastily-scrawled, abrupt letter is very discourteous, and care should be taken to write neat and orderly letters, however brief they may be.

Try to cultivate a legible style of handwriting, and use good, plain stationery. The envelopes and paper should match, while the handwriting should be free from unnecessary flourishes. In correspondence of *any* kind—business or social—the signature should always be written very clearly.

If a letter runs to more than two pages, the pages should be numbered so that the recipient may read on without any trouble. The writing should always run the same way of the paper.

The address and the date should always be stated,

and care should be taken in the body of the letter where days or dates are concerned. If you wish to meet a friend on the following day, for example, make it clear which day that is, otherwise he may be uncertain whether the "to-morrow" is the day after you wrote the letter, or the day after he receives it. It is correct, therefore, to write as follows:—

"I will meet you to-morrow (Wednesday)."

If the meeting is to take place at a more future date, mention that date:

"I will meet you on Saturday, July 31."

Forms of Address

It is customary now in all social correspondence to address a man as "Esquire"—"Mr" being left more for business correspondence. When writing to a married lady, use her husband's Christian name or initial, not her own. Elsie Smith, wife of John Smith, would therefore be addressed as

MRS JOHN SMITH, or MRS J. SMITH.

The accepted forms of address where people of rank or title are concerned appear in a later chapter.

The stamp should always be placed on the envelope upright, in the top right-hand corner. And the flap of the envelope should not be fastened with sealing-wax or stamp-edging—except, perhaps, in the case of a registered letter. To seal a letter is uncomplimentary to the other members of the household where the recipient lives.

When a letter asking for information or any favour is written, a stamp or stamped addressed envelope should be enclosed. Such a letter may be typewritten if desired, but ordinary social correspondence should always be written in ink.

The closing phrases most in use are the following: When writing to friends, "Yours sincerely," or "Yours most sincerely"; to acquaintances, "Yours truly"; and in business communications, "Yours faithfully."

Nothing of a personal or confidential nature should ever be written on a postcard. The usual form of opening, "Dear——," should be omitted, as also should be the closing phrase, "Yours sincerely."

" Third-person " Communications

Third-person communications are rare now, except in the case of invitations. Where a communication is received in the third person, it should usually be answered in the same manner. Here is an example of an invitation written in the third person:—

Mr and Mrs John Smith request the pleasure of
Mr Brown's Company at Dinner
on Saturday, July 31st, at 8 o'clock.

101 *Graham Avenue.*   *R.S.V.P.*

The reply should be written in the following
manner:—

Mr Brown has much pleasure in accepting Mr and
Mrs Smith's kind invitation to Dinner on July 31st.

Letters of Condolence

It is necessary that certain letters be written on
particular occasions.   Thus, in the event of a death
occurring in a friend's family, a letter of condolence
should always be sent.

Such a letter should be very brief; a few words
of sincere sympathy convey your feelings much
better than a lengthy epistle.   Below is a specimen
letter of this nature, alternative words being shown
so that the writer may choose those words which
the circumstances suggest are most suitable.

"MY DEAR——,

"I am $\left\{\begin{array}{l}\text{deeply}\\\text{sincerely}\end{array}\right\}$ $\left\{\begin{array}{l}\text{distressed}\\\text{sorry}\end{array}\right\}$ to $\left\{\begin{array}{l}\text{hear}\\\text{learn}\end{array}\right\}$ of the $\left\{\begin{array}{l}\text{great}\\\text{sad}\end{array}\right\}$ $\left\{\begin{array}{l}\text{loss}\\\text{blow}\end{array}\right\}$ you have $\left\{\begin{array}{l}\text{suffered}\\\text{sustained}\end{array}\right\}$ in the $\left\{\begin{array}{l}\text{death}\\\text{passing away}\end{array}\right\}$ of—— Allow me to $\left\{\begin{array}{l}\text{offer}\\\text{tender}\end{array}\right\}$ you my $\left\{\begin{array}{l}\text{heartfelt}\\\text{deepest}\end{array}\right\}$ sympathy.

"Yours   very   sincerely.''

Letters of Congratulation

Letters of congratulation are called for at times, on the announcement of an engagement, for instance. But remember that it is the man who is congratulated; the good fortune is entirely his. A letter to a girl who has become engaged should speak only of the pleasure the news gives you.

Referring to the engagement, to a man friend you should say:

" Allow me to congratulate you upon your engagement to——. You are a very lucky man indeed, Jack. I wish you both long life and every possible happiness."

To the girl:

" I am delighted to hear of the news of your engagement to Jack. I congratulate him on his choice—and on his good fortune, and I hope you will both be very, very happy."

On the occasion of a birth, write to the father as follows:

" Heartiest congratulations on the birth of your son. I trust that your wife and the boy are both getting on splendidly.

" Please convey my congratulations and very best wishes to your wife."

CHAPTER XIII

THE ENGAGEMENT

Newspaper Announcements—Engagement Parties—The
Parents—Holidays—Broken Engagements

IF you contemplate becoming engaged, remember
it will not be correct for you to buy the ring without
first consulting the lady as to the style she would
prefer. She may either state her preference, or
accompany you to make the purchase. In either
case, every effort must be made to meet her wishes.

It is not very often that a young man is now called
upon to "interview" the girl's father. It will be
a compliment to him, however, if you provide an
opportunity for him to discuss your affairs with you
if he so wishes.

If you wish to announce the engagement in a local
or other paper, the announcement should take the
following form:—

"*A marriage has been arranged and will shortly
take place between Mr John Smith, son of Mr Robert
Smith, of The Myrtles, Grange Road, and Elsie,
daughter of Mr Charles Brown, of 70, New Crescent.*"

If the date of the wedding has been settled when the announcement is made, it should be included, and the words "will shortly take place" omitted.

The announcement may only be made with the girl's full consent, and a man should not allow it to be published without first consulting her.

Sometimes an engagement is celebrated by a small dinner or other function. Invitations should be issued by the girl's parents, but no reference should be made on the invitation to the reason for the function. The announcement is made indirectly, by the host and hostess introducing, and speaking of, the young man as their future son-in-law. No formal speeches are made, as a rule.

The Parents

If at the time the engagement is to be entered upon the lady is living away from home, you should write to her father stating that you and his daughter propose shortly to become engaged, and expressing the hope that the step meets with his approval.

If your home is distant from that of the lady you should ask your mother to invite the girl to stay with her for a convenient period.

If, again, the two families live in different parts of the country, efforts should be made to arrange a visit so that they may meet.

Frequently a young couple will wish to go away

together for their holidays.   This is now an accepted custom, but should the parents raise any objection, efforts should be made to meet it.   The difficulty can often be overcome by inviting another couple to share the holiday, or, if this is not possible, by the man staying at a different house.

It is understood that an engaged couple wish to spend a deal of time and attention on each other. But it is bad form for them to be so engrossed in each other that other friends are ignored, or that they make themselves in any way conspicuous.

Broken Engagements

If an engagement is broken off, all presents should be returned, including the ring.

Should matters have gone so far that any announcements have been made or invitations issued, these must immediately be cancelled, either by letter, or by the publication of the following notification:—

" *The marriage arranged between Mr John Smith and Miss Elsie Brown will not take place.*"

It is a chivalrous action for the man, if possible, to take the blame for the broken engagement.   If he cannot do this, he should be certain to refrain from any slighting comments on the girl.

CHAPTER XIV

THE BRIDEGROOM

The Banns—Marriage by Licence—The Wedding Expenses
—The Ceremony—Signing the Register—Toasts at the
Wedding Breakfast—The Bridegroom's Speech—The
Bride's Father

BEFORE a marriage can take place according to
Church of England rites, banns must be published
prior to the marriage for three consecutive Sundays.
The banns are published in the parish church of
the parish in which the couple live. If they live
in different parishes, the banns must be published
in each.

At least a week before the first Sunday on which
the banns are to be published, notice should be
given to the clergyman of the parish, or of both
parishes. The marriage can take place in either of
the churches where the banns were called, presuming
that the couple live in different parishes, but the
minister performing the ceremony will require a
certificate that the banns have duly been published
in the second parish church. The clergyman concerned will provide this certificate.

The marriage must take place within three months of the calling of the banns, or the banns have to be published again.

When arranging for the publication of the banns, arrangements should also be made with the minister regarding the day and time for the ceremony, so that invitations may be sent out in good time.

When the desire is to marry in a Nonconformist church or in a register office, a licence must be obtained from the registrar of the district. Only one notice is necessary, whether the couple live in the same or different districts, but a fifteen-days' residential qualification is necessary.

In the case of a register-office marriage, the time and date should be arranged with the registrar when the notice is given, while for a marriage in a Nonconformist church the minister of the church concerned should be visited.

When any question arises as to whether the marriage shall take place in a church or register office, the wishes of the lady should be the first consideration.

The arrangements for the ceremony having been made, invitations are then sent out. These invitations are issued by the parents of the bride-to-be, and you should hand them a list of the guests you would like invited. The list is usually drawn up after consultation with the lady. You must also appoint your best man. Although usually preferred, it is not essential for him to be an unmarried man.

The Financial Arrangements

All matters in connection with the reception after the wedding are in the hands of the bride's parents, and you should leave them a free hand unless invited to assist. The parents pay all expenses of the reception. They also arrange for the motor-cars or other conveyances used to take the bride and bridesmaids to the wedding, and pay for them.

You pay for your own conveyance to the church and for the conveyance in which you leave the house after the reception.

It is your privilege to provide and pay for the flowers for the bride and bridesmaids. You should also provide a little gift for each of the bridesmaids —the bride will advise you what to buy. These gifts should be delivered to the bridesmaids not later than the day before the wedding.

You will also buy the ring and a wedding present for your bride.

You are responsible for the clergyman's fee and any other fees connected with the wedding, providing your best man beforehand with the necessary funds with which to pay these fees.

Suggestions as to the most suitable dress for the occasion appear in a subsequent chapter.

The Ceremony

Be sure to arrive at the church in good time, and take a seat near the chancel to await the coming of the bride. When she arrives at the door of the church, take your place near the chancel steps, the best man a little behind you on your right hand. The bride will take her place on your left.

The ceremony is beautifully simple, and the officiating clergyman will tell you exactly what to do. There is no need for the slightest nervousness.

After the ceremony is completed, offer your left arm to your wife, and follow the clergyman to the vestry to sign the register. The best man, chief bridesmaid, and the bride's parents will follow you. After the register is signed, congratulations are given, but you must be the first to kiss the bride!

Your wife then takes your left arm, and you pass out of the church to face your waiting friends! Hand your wife into the vehicle, take your seat— and *that* part of the wedding is over.

When there is a sit-down meal after the wedding, you and your bride will occupy the seats of honour at the top of the table. Your bride will be on your left, her father on her left, her mother on your right.

The Bridegroom's Speech

It is not usual for there to be a number of toasts, but all present will drink the health of your bride and yourself. This toast is usually proposed by an intimate family friend.

You have to reply. To make a speech is rather an ordeal for many men, but fortunately only a brief speech is expected of a bridegroom.

The following indicates the lines upon which a bridegroom's speech usually runs:—

"Ladies and Gentlemen—

"Let me thank you very sincerely indeed, on behalf of my wife and myself, for the warm-hearted way in which you have just wished us good health and happiness. I can hardly find words to say how very deeply we appreciate the kind sentiments expressed towards us when the toast was being proposed.

"As you all will know, this is a wonderfully happy day for us—for me, in particular; and our happiness is made still greater by the fact that we have so many of our dear old friends here to wish us 'good luck.' With so many friends round us, with so many true and sincere wishes expressed for our future happiness, my wife and I start our days of married life together under the happiest circumstances possible.

"One word more. I cannot refrain from taking advantage of this opportunity to thank you all for the beautiful presents you have given us. Every one of these beautiful gifts will find an honoured place in our home, and we shall feel, whenever we look at one of the gifts, that it brought with it, not only for this day but for all time, the sincerest wishes of the friend concerned that happiness and good fortune might always be ours.

"From the bottom of our hearts we thank you for all you have done towards making this day so wonderfully happy for us both."

Sometimes the bridegroom then proposes the health of the bridesmaids, and after the best man has responded on their behalf the time has come to cut the cake.

The bride cuts the first slice, with your help if necessary, after which pieces are distributed to all present.

After this, you and your bride get ready to depart for the honeymoon.

The Bride's Father

Usually, the bride is "given away" by her father. A word as to the father's part in the ceremony may not therefore be out of place.

The father accompanies the bride to the church. On arrival at the porch he offers the bride his right arm, and then, followed by the bridesmaids, he and the bride walk up the aisle. When the bride has taken her place at the chancel steps, he remains a little in the rear, on the bride's left hand.

Here he remains until the clergyman asks who gives away the bride. He steps forward to make reply, and then resumes his former position.

After the register has been signed, the bride's father and mother return to the house in the car immediately following that of the bride and bridegroom. They remain near the door to greet the guests before they pass into the reception. The bride's father accompanies the bridegroom's mother into the breakfast, and he takes his seat on the left of the bride.

Finally, the bride's parents are at hand to say good-bye when the guests are leaving.

The bridegroom's father has no special duty beyond that of taking the bride's mother into the breakfast.

CHAPTER XV

DUTIES OF THE BEST MAN

Before the Ceremony—At the Church—The Chief Brides-
    maid—The Wedding Breakfast—The Best Man's
    Speech—Other Duties

THE best man has many duties to perform on the day of the wedding. If you are asked to act in this capacity, however, and wish to play your part thoroughly, you will find that there are many ways in which you can help well before the actual day.

If possible, you should place your spare time at the disposal of your friend several days beforehand. He will have a great many things to attend to, and you may be able to save him a deal of worry and a last-minute rush.

On the wedding-day you should be with the bridegroom at an early hour, to help him in any way possible, and to see that he is ready to leave for the church in good time.

Before setting out, make sure that the ring is safely in your possession. Take charge of any certificates or other papers required, and see if your friend has any special wishes with regard to the ceremony or special guests.

The bridegroom should provide you, beforehand, with the necessary money to pay all fees and tips.

At the Church

You should arrive at the church with the bridegroom fully fifteen minutes before the bride is due —the bride being due to arrive at the actual time fixed for the ceremony. During this period, if possible, pay the fees, thus saving time after the ceremony.

One of your duties is to look after the bridegroom's hat and gloves. Place them in some convenient spot where you can get them easily and quickly when the ceremony is over.

A few minutes before the bride is due, the bridegroom and yourself should take seats in the front row on the right-hand side of the church.

As soon as the bride reaches the church door, the groom will take his place at the right of the chancel steps, and you will stand, a little behind him, to his right.

All you have to do during the ceremony is to hand over the ring at the correct moment. Have it quite ready, so that there is no fumbling or delay.

At the conclusion of the ceremony, you offer your left arm to the chief bridesmaid—who is your special "partner" during the rest of the day's proceedings—and follow the newly-married couple into the vestry to sign the register.

After the signing of the register, you give the bridegroom his hat and gloves, and see the couple into their carriage. You then see the bride's parents into their conveyance, and follow in the next carriage with the chief bridesmaid and any other guests for whom there may be room.

At the breakfast you do all you can to assist in the smooth running of affairs. You help to get the guests seated, and see that their needs are supplied.

The Best Man's Speech

Your next duty is to respond to the toast of the bridesmaids. Your speech should be as light as possible, and, although you are responding for the bridesmaids, your remarks should be very complimentary towards them.

The following shows the usual tone of speeches of this nature:—

"Ladies and Gentlemen,—

"Among the many pleasant duties I have had an opportunity to perform to-day, none could be more pleasant than this—to respond to your very cordial toast of the bridesmaids.

"No one has ever been able to discover, I understand,

just why there are bridesmaids at a wedding. But to-day I claim to have found the reason. They are present so that, with the bride, they may make the ceremony delightful to the eye. And to-day the bridesmaids have played their part in a manner in which no words of mine can do justice.

" You will easily understand that I count it a great privilege to be allowed to speak on behalf of these ladies ; and the privilege more than compensates me for the task I have had to prevent the bridegroom from getting nervous—for, as you know, the bridegroom is always pictured as a particularly nervous subject.

" But bridesmaids are never nervous. Why should they be ? If I were a girl and had the pleasure to be a bridesmaid, and if I knew that I made a charming picture, I shouldn't be nervous, I can assure you.

" However, ladies and gentlemen, all I have to do really is to thank you for your toast. On behalf of the bridesmaids I do thank you—very sincerely indeed. I know, too, that I may say on their behalf that, like the rest of us, they are delighted to be taking part in the events of this very, very happy day."

Sometimes the best man accompanies the newly-married couple to the station, to obtain the tickets if these have not already been purchased, and to see to the disposal of their luggage. Many couples prefer to go alone, however, and you should ascertain the bridegroom's wishes in this matter.   In any case you should see that the car is ready at the right time to take the couple to the station, and you should see to the disposal of any luggage they may be taking with them.

If you remain behind, you should, with the help of the chief bridesmaid, endeavour to keep amused any guests who may be staying for a time.

Suggestions as to the most suitable style of clothing for the occasion appear in the next chapter.

CHAPTER XVI

MATTERS OF DRESS

The Well-dressed Man—Business Dress—Flannels—Evening Dress—Dress for Dances—Tying a Bow—Dress for a Wedding

THE prevailing fashion in men's dress varies slightly from time to time in such minor details as the number of buttons on a coat, the colour of the socks, or the shape of the collar. Apart from such details, our style of clothing changes very little at any time, and the passing fashions but slightly affect the established rules for good and correct dressing.

Neat, quiet, and suitable; those three words describe the clothing of the well-dressed man.

It is a true saying that a man is well dressed when you do not notice what he has on. If a man is so clad as to be conspicuous, it is evident that his taste has run a little off the rails.

Suitability is as important as neatness; it is essential to wear clothes suitable for the occasion. To take an extreme example, a man would not look well in a plus-fours suit at a dance, however good the suit might be in itself in cut and material.

Business Dress

So far as business clothing is concerned, a man's work or profession very largely decides what he should wear. But even where a man's occupation is such that he is more or less at liberty to dress as he pleases, there is still some sort of convention to follow.

The accepted style of dress for the young man in business is either a black coat and vest worn with striped trousers, or a lounge suit cut in the prevailing fashion. The lounge suit should be of some dark material, for reasons of economy as well as suitability. Unless very well cared for, and worn in exchange with one or two other suits, a light-coloured material soon begins to look shabby.

With a lounge suit, either a double or a wing collar is correct, though with the black coat a wing collar is more "dressy." Soft collars should not be worn during business hours.

Grey flannel trousers are still very popular for week-end and holiday wear, but the once almost universal sports jacket has lost favour. An odd lounge jacket, or else a blazer, should be worn with flannels, though, strictly, the blazer should be worn only with white flannels.

When a shirt with an attached collar is worn—
for cricket, tennis, boating, or the beach—a tie is
not required. If you do not care to appear without
a tie, you should wear an ordinary soft shirt with a
separate soft collar.

Evening Dress

The dinner jacket has become extremely popular
during the last few years, and it is now regarded
as being quite suitable wear for all but the most
formal occasions.

The "sundries" worn with the dinner jacket differ
from those worn with the swallow-tail, and these
differences must be kept well in mind. With the
swallow-tail, for example, either a black or a white
bow may be worn, but with the dinner jacket only
a black bow is in order.

Again, with the tail coat either a black or white
waistcoat may be worn. Efforts have been made
to popularise the wearing of a white waistcoat with
a dinner jacket. But the efforts have not met with
very much success, and you are advised to abide
by the old order of a black waistcoat with a dinner
jacket. If, however, you do wear a white waistcoat, remember that a black bow must still be
worn.

Almost any kind of white shirt may be worn with
a dinner jacket—soft-pleated, silken, or "hard-

boiled," but a stiff shirt should be worn with full dress. Occasionally a man will wish to wear one of the cream, soft-fronted, silk shirts which are now rather popular. A shirt of this kind, however, should not be worn with a white waistcoat. There is no strict rule as to the number of studs worn in the front. Fashion favours one style more than another at times, but in the main you can wear the style which most pleases you.

Lace-up patent leather shoes should be worn with either a dinner jacket or full evening dress.

Dances

At most ordinary small dances either a dinner jacket or full evening dress is permissible. You may therefore be in doubt as to whether you will wear full dress or not. If you are taking a partner you should follow her lead. If she will be wearing full evening dress, you should do likewise, but if she is going in "a little frock" the dinner jacket is more suitable.

Gloves are rarely worn at any dances now except, perhaps, in the case of a large ball or big private dance.

One other thing: Whether you are wearing a white or black bow, remember that it must be tied by hand. "Made up" bows are taboo. It is quite easy to tie a bow, but should you be one of the many men who find the task difficult, the diagrams below will help you.

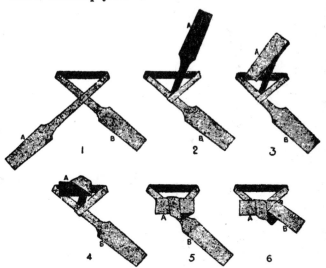

The easiest way in which to tie a dress bow.

Weddings

The style of dress worn by a bridegroom depends very largely upon that worn by the bride. When the bride is appearing in a full bridal toilette, the bridegroom should wear a morning coat, striped trousers, patent leather shoes, white spats, and silk hat.

For less formal occasions, where the bride is wearing less elaborate clothing, a black coat and vest, striped trousers, black leather shoes, and a bowler hat comprise a suitable turn-out. The best man takes his cue from the bridegroom, and should so far as possible wear similar clothing. He should not wear more elaborate garb than the bridegroom. If, for example, the bridegroom is wearing a lounge suit, the best man should not appear in a morning coat and silk hat.

Whatever style of suit is worn, a small button-hole, consisting of one white flower, is customary. If the suit has a breast pocket, a white handkerchief should show just above the top of the pocket, while gloves, preferably of grey suède, should always be carried.

On no occasion should a man wear much jewellery. The most he should ever wear is one ring, preferably a plain gold signet ring without a stone, a slender watch-chain, and a neat tie-pin—though, as a matter of fact, pins are rarely worn nowadays.

The way in which a man wears his clothes is of the utmost importance. If you have a nice crease in your trousers, are careful to see that your suit is well brushed, and that your linen is clean, you will always have a well-groomed, smart appearance.

CHAPTER XVII

TRAVELLING BY TRAIN

The Other Passengers—Conversation—Lady Passengers
—Luggage—Smoking—The Window Seat

A CONVERSATION does much to lighten the tedium of a long railway journey, and there is no reason why a remark should not be addressed to the man in the opposite corner or next to you in the compartment.

If the passenger addressed does not wish to talk he will make this evident from his answer. No further comments should then be passed. It is incorrect to try to force a conversation upon anyone.

If a conversation does develop from your remark about the weather or the scenery, well and good. The only point is that the conversation must be kept impersonal. You should not inquire into the other man's movements or affairs, and you should not discuss your own.

A lady passenger should not be addressed so directly. It is in order to pay her formal little courtesies—to open the door, adjust the window, offer the loan of a paper or magazine, or to assist in the disposal of luggage. But a small action of this kind does not entitle you to start a conversation, unless the lady shows she will have no objection to passing the time in this manner.

To talk with a lady passenger does not give you the right to offer to buy papers or refreshments for her, to tip the porter on her behalf, or to make any other expenditure.

General Hints

Dispose of your luggage in such a way that it does not inconvenience other passengers. It is unfair to the others to take into a carriage bulky bags or packages which should really be in the guard's van.

Strictly, it is not correct to eat in a railway carriage. On a long journey, however, especially where there is no restaurant car, the strict rule is rarely adhered to, while at times tea is served in the carriages by the refreshment staff of the train. But in no circumstances should you eat or drink anything of such a nature as to be objectionable to other passengers.

You have a perfect right to smoke in a smoking compartment, but if there are ladies in the carriage it is courteous to ask their permission first.

You should not smoke in such a way that the smoke is blown into the faces of other passengers; nor should you smoke a strong pipe or strong tobacco.

Parents travelling with children should see that the children do not interfere with the comfort of others in the compartment.

It is accepted that the passenger occupying the window seat facing the engine has "control" of the window.   If seated in another part of the compartment you should not raise or lower the window without a "Do you mind?" to this passenger.

If you occupy the window seat, you should not alter the position of the window purely for your own comfort.   A word of inquiry should be addressed to passengers seated near.

Provided there is room elsewhere, you should not enter a compartment in which a lady is seated alone.

CHAPTER XVIII

BOARDING-HOUSES AND HOTELS

Boarding-houses—Use of the Bathroom—The Servants
—The other Guests—Hotels—Evening Dress

MOST boarding-houses, especially those which cater for holiday-makers, are run on fairly free-and-easy lines. Generally there are but few rules and regulations, but because they are so few especial care should be taken to abide by them.

In most houses, for example, there is a stated closing time. There are also stated hours during which visitors may use the bathroom. Notice of these hours will generally be found in the bedroom, and attention should be paid to them. In certain cases it may be necessary to make arrangements overnight when a hot bath is required. Where there is limited bathroom accommodation do not occupy the bathroom for an unnecessarily long time. Remember the other visitors.

Usually, the hours at which meals are served will also be found posted up in the bedroom. If not so shown, the hours should be ascertained

straight away. The smooth-running of the house
depends to a large extent on the punctuality of
guests at meal times, and to be late is extremely
thoughtless.

If you are a newcomer and enter the common
sitting-room, it is correct for you to pass the time
of day with those present. Introductions are not
necessary, though the landlady will probably introduce you in a general way if she happens to be
in the room.

Try to fall in with the general "temperament"
of the house. If most of the guests happen to
be quiet, elderly people who wish to spend their
time while indoors in writing letters or reading,
it is discourteous to be unnecessarily boisterous or
noisy.

Do not treat the servants in an off-handed manner,
and do not discuss the shortcomings of the house,
real or imaginary, with the other guests. If you
have cause for complaint, such complaint should
be made in the proper quarter.

You should show just the right degree of friendliness towards the other guests—you should not be
stand-offish, nor effusive. Don't join a clique.
Occasionally in a boarding-house a small party will
keep themselves aloof from the rest of the guests,
but you should not encourage such behaviour by
joining them.

7

If a party is made up from the house for any excursion, it is graceful to join in if invited to do so. You should not, however, offer to pay the expenses of any lady in the party if you are only boarding-house friends.

Towards the end of your stay, let the landlady know at what time you will be leaving. This will help her with regard to the arrangements for meals. You should vacate your room by twelve noon on the day of departure, unless an alternative arrangement is made, the incoming occupant having a right to possession at that time.

Hotels

Upon arriving at an hotel you should go direct to the office to sign the register and receive the key of your room.

There is not usually the same degree of friendliness between the guests in an hotel as in a boarding-house. If you share a table, however, you should pass the time of day with others seated at it. Conversation may ensue if there is a mutual desire for it.

Conversation is general, as a rule, in the lounge or smoking-room; and if there is a dance it will be quite in order for you to approach any lady present without the formality of an introduction.

Evening dress is not general, though in some smart establishments guests are expected to wear it. If you intend to stay in a large hotel it may be as well either to take evening dress with you, or to find out if it is usually worn when booking your room, presuming you book in advance.

CHAPTER XIX

TIPPING

Tea-rooms and Restaurants—Hotels—Boarding-houses
—A Friend's Servants—Porters and Others

WHETHER we approve of the tipping system or not, we have to accept it as an established custom, upon which many workers—waiters, waitresses, and chamber-maids, for instance—depend for the main part of their earnings.   There is no need for you to tip lavishly because of this fact, but you should give when necessary in an ungrudging manner and without being patronising.

The amount given as a tip in a tea-room or restaurant is usually based on the amount of the bill—about 10 per cent. being adequate.   If the bill comes to five shillings, a sixpenny tip would be correct; if ten shillings, one shilling should be given; and so on.

After a stay in a medium-sized hotel, a similar percentage of the bill should be given to the staff. If your bill comes to £5, tips to the amount of ten shillings should be adequate.

The amount should be divided between the waiter at your table, the head waiter, chamber-maid, hall porter, and "boots," in the following proportion: Waiter, three shillings; head waiter, chamber-maid, and hall porter, two shillings each; boots, one shilling.

In a boarding-house the staff is usually much smaller, and probably there will be only a waitress and chamber-maid to tip. After a fortnight's stay, five shillings for the waitress and half-a-crown for the chamber-maid will do very well.

Sometimes in a boarding-house a member of the family will wait on you at table. You must then use your discretion whether the tip shall be in cash or in the form of a box of chocolates or other gift.

Hotels

In a large London hotel a rather higher percentage of the amount of the bill may be necessary, to tip the servants, in addition to those mentioned, who will appear when you are leaving!

It is not correct to tip the servants in any club which you may visit as a friend of a member. Nor should you tip the servants in a friend's house after an ordinary call or a dinner or other party. Exception to the latter rule may be made, however, if the servant renders you a special and personal service, such as finding you a taxi. In this case a small gratuity will not be out of place.

After a stay in a friend's house you should tip the servants, especially those who have ministered directly to your comfort.

You should never try to force a tip upon anyone who is unready to accept it. And you should have the moral courage to withhold a tip, however much it may be expected, if you do not feel that you have had the care, civility, or attention which is your due.

Among others, in addition to those already mentioned, who normally expect a tip for services, are the attendants in theatre and dance-hall cloak-rooms, railway-porters, taxi - drivers, and hair-dressers. The amount given should, of course, depend on the service rendered, but, generally speaking, anything from threepence to one shilling is adequate.

CHAPTER XX

SOME SPECIAL OCCASIONS

Christenings — Newspaper Announcements — Christening Receptions—Silver Weddings—Golding Weddings— Bereavements—Mourning Dress

Christenings

If you hear of the arrival of a little stranger in a friend's household you should immediately send a note of congratulation to the parents.

About a week after the event you may call at the house to inquire as to the progress of the mother and child, and to leave a few flowers.

When the time for christening comes along, you should send some small gift for the child, especially if you have been invited to become a godfather.

In the case of a boy there should be at least two godfathers and a godmother; for a girl, one godfather and two or more godmothers.

Should the event occur in your household, and you wish to make an announcement in the local paper, the announcement should take the following form:—

Birth

On the 1st inst., at 101, Graham Avenue,
the wife of John Smith, a daughter.

Information must be supplied to the local registrar within forty-two days of the event.

Arrangements must be made with the clergyman of the church in which the christening is to take place. No fee is charged, but a donation should be made to one of the church funds. Occasionally a reception will be held after the christening, in which case it is a graceful little act to invite the clergyman who officiated.

Silver Weddings

A silver wedding is the twenty-fifth anniversary of a couple's marriage, and sometimes the occasion is marked by a little celebration.

If cards of invitation are issued they are printed in silver. Each guest invited sends some small present. The present need not be elaborate or costly, but it must be an article of silver.

If a tea or dinner-party is given, a wedding-cake, ornamented with silver flowers, will appear on the table. The health of the couple will be proposed by an old friend, the husband will respond for himself and his wife, and then the cake will be cut.

Golden-wedding celebrations, marking the fiftieth anniversary, are not of such frequent occurrence. As the couple are necessarily getting on in years, a party is unusual.

Should you know a couple who have reached the golden-wedding date, be sure to send them congratulations. You are not expected to make a gift of anything golden, but a few flowers or some such trifle should be left at the house.

Bereavements

Should a death occur in the family of a friend, a message of condolence should be sent, and, on the day of the funeral, a wreath should be delivered at the house, unless a definite wish has been expressed that there shall be no flowers. The wreath need not necessarily consist of white flowers.

A mourning card, such as may be obtained at a stationer's, or a black-edged postcard, should be attached, bearing your name.

If you are asked to attend the funeral you must do so in dark, if not in black, clothes, whether a relation or not. Your suit, boots, hat, and gloves should all be dark or black; the tie must be black, while the shirt and handkerchief should be plain white. Black-bordered handkerchiefs are not now used, while mourning-bands for the hat are also going out of use. The arm-band has given place to a small piece of black material sewn on the coat sleeve.

If only a friend of the family, and not a relation, you should remain in the background as much as possible.

Men do not wear mourning for a very long period, even when the bereavement occurs in their own family, except when widowed. A widower usually wears black clothes for a short time, following his mourning clothes with a suit of dark material.

CHAPTER XXI

WRITTEN FORMS OF ADDRESS

Medical Men—The Clergy—The Bar—Army and Navy
Officers—Knights and Baronets—Other Men of Title
—The Royal Family—Courtesy Titles—Other Forms
of Address

IT is very desirable when writing to professional men, or to people of title, that the correct form of address be used on the envelope and in the letter itself.

The following list of accepted forms of address is therefore inserted, in a convenient form, for reference. In addition to the correct form for the envelope, the most suitable opening and closing phrases are also mentioned where these differ from those in general use.

Medical Men

The form of address in this case depends largely upon whether the medical man is a surgeon or a physician. A surgeon is addressed as "Esq." on the envelope, followed by any letters to which he may be entitled, thus:

A. BROWN, ESQ., F.R.C.S.

A physician should be addressed by the abbreviation "Dr." In any instance where you are in doubt use this form.

The letter should start "Dear Sir" or "Dear Mr Brown" in the case of a surgeon, and "Dear Sir" or "Dear Dr Brown" in the case of a physician.

"Yours faithfully" is the usual closing phrase, unless you are on terms of friendship which justify the use of the phrase "Yours sincerely."

The Clergy

An Archbishop should be given the name of his See—thus: "His Grace the Lord Archbishop of Canterbury"; a Bishop as "The Right Rev. the Lord Bishop of London"; a Dean as "The Very Rev. the Dean of Durham."

In a letter, an Archbishop should be addressed as "Your Grace," and it should end "Your Grace's most obedient servant." A Bishop is addressed as "My Lord," the closing phrase being "I am, my Lord, your obedient servant." A letter to a Dean should begin "Mr Dean" or "Reverend Sir," and end "I remain, Reverend Sir, your obedient servant."

Letters to other members of the clergy are addressed as "Reverend." The Christian name or initial should always be given: "Rev. Arthur Brown"—not simply "Rev. Brown." The letter should begin "Reverend Sir," unless you are on terms of friendship, in which case the usual phrase "Dear Mr Brown" should be used. The closing phrases in general use may be employed here.

The Bar

Justices of the Peace are addressed in the usual way, with the letters J.P. added:

A. BROWN, ESQ., J.P.

Judges are addressed by their title "Mr Justice Brown." The Lord Chancellor is addressed as "The Rt. Hon. the Lord High Chancellor" and the Lord Chief Justice as "The Rt. Hon. the Lord Chief Justice."

Letters to ordinary members of the Bar, and to other professional men, follow the usual form.

Army and Navy Officers

The rank should be given on the envelope in the case of officers in either the Army or the Navy. Where the rank is Major-General, Lieutenant-Colonel, or Vice-Admiral, the full rank—"General," "Colonel," or "Admiral"—should be given in all social correspondence.

An officer below the rank of Captain in the Army, or Commander in the Navy, is addressed as "Mr" in the letter itself. The envelope should state the rank if the letter is being sent to a barracks or ship, but "Esq." should be used if the officer is away from his place of duty.

Knights and Baronets

A gentleman with either of these titles should be addressed on the envelope as "Sir." In the case of Baronet, the abbreviation "Bt." should appear after the name:

SIR ARTHUR BROWN, BT.

It may be mentioned in passing that the abbreviation "Bt." should be used in preference to "Bart.," the shorter form being preferred by the Society of Baronets, which exists to protect the rights and privileges of holders of that title.

The wife of a Knight or Baronet is addressed by the title "Lady." When the titled daughter of a peer marries a commoner she retains her title.

Other Men of Title

A letter to a Duke of the Royal Family should be addressed to "His Royal Highness the Duke of Blankshire." The foregoing should appear at the head of the letter, which should commence with the word "Sir." The closing phrase is "I have the honour to remain, Sir, your most obedient servant."

A Duke not of the Royal Family should be addressed as "His Grace the Duke of Blankshire." In the letter the phrase "My Lord Duke" should be used. The closing phrase is "I have the honour to be your Grace's obedient servant."

A Marquis is addressed as " The Most Honourable

the Marquis of Blankshire," an Earl as "The Right Honourable the Earl of Blankshire," and a Viscount as "The Right Honourable Viscount Blankshire." In each case the opening is "My Lord," and the closing phrase "I have the honour to be, my Lord, your obedient servant."

The Royal Family

A letter to the King should be addressed to " His Majesty the King." The letter should begin " May it please your Majesty," and end with " I have the honour to remain your Majesty's loyal subject and faithful servant." A letter to the Queen should be addressed to " Her Majesty the Queen." The opening and closing phrases should be as above.

A letter to the Prince of Wales (if there is a holder of this title) should be addressed to " His Royal Highness the Prince of Wales." The opening is either " Sir " or " May it please your Royal Highness," and the closing phrase " I have the honour to remain your Royal Highness's most obedient servant."

Courtesy Titles

The eldest son of a Duke takes by courtesy one of his father's secondary titles, by which he should be addressed. Other sons have the title "Lord" prefixed to their Christian name—"Lord Arthur ——." The daughter of a Duke similarly has the title "Lady" prefixed to her Christian name.

The same remarks apply to the sons and daughters of an Earl, except that a younger son would be addressed as "The Hon. Arthur Brown."

The sons and daughters of a Viscount are all addressed as "The Hon."

It should be noted that in these courtesy titles the Christian name is always retained. It would not be correct to address the "Lady Alice Brown" as "Lady Brown."

Other Forms of Address

A Lord Mayor is addressed as "The Lord Mayor of——," though the Lord Mayors of London, York, and Belfast, and the Lord Provosts of Edinburgh and Glasgow are entitled to the prefix of "Right Honourable." The letter should begin "My Lord," and end "I remain your Lordship's obedient servant." A Mayor is usually addressed simply as "The Mayor of——."

Letters to Members of Parliament are addressed in the usual way, with the letters "M.P." after the name:

A. BROWN, ESQ., M.P.

If the gentleman concerned possesses any professional distinction, the letters "M.P." come last, as:

A. BROWN, ESQ., M.D., M.P.

Members of town and other local councils are addressed formally as "Mr Councillor."

CHAPTER XXII

PERSONAL FORMS OF ADDRESS

Titled People—Royal Family—Clergy—Army and
Navy Officers—Pronunciation of Surnames

A BRIEF reference may well be made to the personal
forms of address in use, in order that no one may
feel awkward when in the company of persons
holding high rank or title.

A Baronet or Knight is addressed by his title and
Christian name: "Sir John"; his wife is addressed
as "Lady——" by her social equals and as "Your
Ladyship" or "My Lady" by others.

A Duke or Duchess is usually addressed as "Your
Grace"; a Marquis or Earl as "Your Lordship"
or "My Lord." A Marchioness or Countess is
addressed as "Your Ladyship" or "My Lady."

An Earl or Marquis is usually referred to as
"Lord——" by social equals.

The King and Queen are addressed as "Your
Majesty," though anyone in closer contact uses the
terms "Sir" and "Madam." The Prince of Wales
is spoken to as "Your Royal Highness" or "Sir."

Foreign noblemen are generally addressed by their ordinary full title.

The Clergy and Others

An Archbishop is addressed as "Your Grace"; a Bishop as "My Lord"; a Dean is addressed by his clerical title and surname, as also is an Archdeacon, while other clergymen are addressed as "Mr——" except in cases where the term "Father" is usual.

Officers in the Army or Navy are addressed by their rank and surname. A Lieutenant in the Army, however, is addressed as "Mr——," and, as in the written form of address, a Lieutenant-Colonel is given the full rank "Colonel."

In none of the cases mentioned does the wife take any title from their husband's office or rank.

Pronouncing Surnames

A little difficulty arises at times owing to the fact that certain surnames are not pronounced as spelt. The following list of surnames, showing the accepted form of pronunciation, may therefore be useful:

SPELLING	PRONUNCIATION
Abergavenny	Abergenny
Arundel	Arrandel
Beaconsfield	Beckonsfield
Beauchamp	Beecham

SPELLING	PRONUNCIATION
Belvoir	Beaver
Berkeley	Barkley
Bethune	Beeton
Bicester	Bister
Blount	Blunt
Blyth or Blythe	Bly
Boleyn	Bullen
Bosanquet	Boo-sanket
Boucher or Bouchier	Bow-cher
Bourke	Burk
Bourne	Burn
Brougham	Broum
Buchan	Buck-an
Charteris	Charters
Chisholm	Chizum
Cholmeley or Cholmondeley	Chumley
Cirencester	Cis-ester
Cockburn	Co-burn
Coghlan	Co-lan
Colquhoun	Kohoon
Coutts	Koots
Cowper	Cooper
Dalziel	Dee-al
Derby	Darby
Devereux	Devereu (*x* not sounded)
Donoghue	Dunnohew
Elgin	Elgin (*g* as in " gate ")
Eyre	Air

SPELLING	PRONUNCIATION
Falconer	Fawkner
Farquhar	Farkwah
Fortescue	Fortiskew
Gifford	Jifford
Gillett	Gillett (*g* as in " gate ")
Gillott	Gillott (*g* as in " gate ")
Glamis	Glarms
Gough	Goff
Gower	Gore
Harcourt	Harkut
Hawarden	Harden
Heathcote	Heth-kut
Hepburn	Hebburn
Hertford	Harford
Home	Hume
Jervis	Jarvis
Knollys	Nowles
Layard	Laird
Lefevre	Le-fever
M'Leod or Macleod	M'Cloud
Mainwaring	Mannering
Majoribanks or Marjoribanks	Marshbanks
Meiklejohn	Micklejohn
Menzies	Myng-ies
Meux	Mews
Monckton	Munkton

SPELLING	PRONUNCIATION
Nigel	Ni-jel
Pepys	Peeps or Pep-is
Ponsonby	Punsonby
Pontefract	Pomfret
Rea	Ray
Ruthven	Riven
St Clair	Sinclair
St John	Sinjin
Sandys	Sands
Scrimgeour	Skrim-jer
Strachan	Strawn
Thynne	Thin
Tyrrwhitt	Tirritt
Urquhart	Erk-wart
Vaughan	Vorn
Villiers	Villers
Waldegrave	Walgrave
Wemyss	Weems

CHAPTER XXIII

THE BACHELOR

Entertaining—Meeting the Family—Without Introduction—Presents

THERE are certain little questions in etiquette which sometimes arise and affect particularly the bachelor —especially when he is living in apartments.

One such question concerns the bachelor who wishes to give a little dinner, tea, or other party in his rooms.

The only way in which you can entertain ladies, if you are placed in these circumstances, is by asking a lady of your own family, or a married lady friend, to act as hostess. You must not invite any married lady to attend without inviting her husband, nor any unmarried girl unless she is to attend with her parents or some other responsible person.

Strictly, it is not correct to take an unmarried girl to dinner or supper in a restaurant unless she is accompanied by a chaperone of some kind. This rule is followed only in very correct circles in these days, however.

Another question which often arises concerns the

man who has become on terms of great friendship
with a girl and wishes to be introduced into her
family circle.

Strictly, again, you should not suggest an invitation, nor is the girl supposed to invite you to
call on her own initiative. The invitation should
come from the girl's mother.

If a girl is living in a boarding-house, you should
call for her only if there is a "common" sitting-
room into which you can be shown while waiting
for her; while if she lives "on her own" in one or
two rooms you should not call for her at all.

Without Introduction

Very often a man will come into contact with a
girl, through business affairs, at a dance or other
function, or under even still less formal circumstances, and a friendship will spring up. There
has been no real introduction, of course.

Convention is less severe on a friendship of this
kind than was formerly the case, and many friendships thus formed have led to courtship and
eventually to happy marriage.

The success of the friendship depends very
largely, indeed, on the man's conduct. Although
the formality of an introduction has been waived,
the man should not relax any other of the con-
ventions in his treatment of the girl.

If a friendship springs up between yourself and a girl you should make it your business to introduce the girl to members of your family, or, at least, to intimate friends at the first opportunity.

Presents

Another little question which occasionally raises doubt in the mind of a bachelor is what he may give to lady friends in the form of presents.

It is not correct for you to give any girl with whom you are only on terms of friendship any article of real value—such as jewellery—of anything that comes under the heading of wearing apparel—such as furs. All that you should give are small things such as chocolates, flowers, books, and the like.

This applies even if the man and girl concerned have passed beyond the stage of ordinary friendship.

When a man becomes engaged, however, it is permissible for him to give his fiancée more valuable and personal gifts, and either jewellery or furs would be quite in order.

CHAPTER XXIV

IN THE HOME

The Need for Courtesy—Husbands and Wives—Children

JUST a few words, in conclusion, regarding etiquette in the home—for there is no other place in which a man shows more definitely whether or not he possesses the instincts of true courtesy. If a man is not considerate and courteous towards his wife, mother, or sisters, as the case may be, the good form he may show outside is merely a veneer, and does not count for very much.

Sometimes a man becomes a little thoughtless of those around him; sometimes a wife will tend to spoil her husband by not expecting, and requiring, from him the same amount of courtesy which she would expect from another man. In either case the position is to be regretted, for no man should allow himself to extend to his wife less courteous treatment than he would extend to any other woman.

Such things as carrying a heavy parcel, opening a door, giving ''right of way'' on the stairs, placing a chair at the table—these and countless other small services are rendered as a matter of course for any lady with whom a man comes in contact; and he should never think twice before performing similar services for the ladies in his own home.

There is no need to labour the point; but just one other aspect of the matter may well be mentioned: Where there are children in the home even greater care should be taken that courtesy between the grown members of the family is evident.

This is because children are so apt to copy the example of their elders. The finest way in which children can be trained to grow up into thoughtful, courteous, and considerate men and women is by surrounding them with those qualities throughout their younger days.

INDEX